D0941259

Wreathmaking
for the first time®

Wreathmaking
for the first time®

Pat Poce & Deon Gooch

Sterling Publishing Co., Inc. New York
A Sterling / Chapelle Book

Chapelle, Ltd.:
 Jo Packham
 Sara Toliver
 Cindy Stoeckl

Editor: Ray Cornia
Art Director: Karla Haberstich
Copy Editor: Marilyn Goff
Photographer: Ryne Hazen for Hazen Photography
Photo Stylist: Suzy Skadburg

Staff: Kelly Ashkettle, Areta Bingham, Anne Bruns, Donna Chambers,
 Emily Frandsen, Lana Hall, Susan Jorgensen, Jennifer Luman,
 Melissa Maynard, Barbara Milburn, Lecia Monsen,
 Kim Taylor, Linda Venditti, Desirée Wybrow

If you have any questions or comments, please contact:
Chapelle, Ltd., Inc., P.O. Box 9252, Ogden, UT 84409
 (801) 621-2777 • (801) 621-2788 Fax
 e-mail: chapelle@chapelleltd.com
 Web sites: www.chapelleltd.com
  www.rubyandbegonia.com

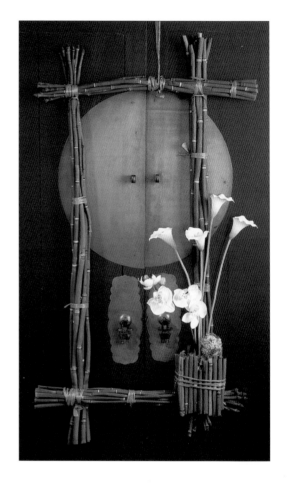

The copy, photographs, instructions, illustrations, designs in this volume are intended for the personal use of the reader and may be reproduced for that purpose only. Any other use, especially commercial use, is forbidden under law without the written permission of the copyright holder.

Every effort has been made to ensure that all information in this book is accurate. However, due to differing conditions, tools, and individual skills, the publisher cannot be responsible for any injuries, losses, and/or other damages which may result from the use of the information in this book.

This volume is meant to stimulate craft ideas. If readers are unfamiliar or not proficient in a skill necessary to attempt a project, we urge that they refer to an instructional book specifically addressing the required technique.

Space would not permit the inclusion of every decorative item photographed for this book, nor could all of the designers be identified. Many of these items are available by calling (801) 334-7829 or by viewing the Ruby & Begonia Web site:

www.rubyandbegonia.com

Library of Congress Cataloging-in-Publication Data:
Poce, Pat.
 Wreathmaking for the first time / Pat Poce & Deon Gooch.
   p. cm.
 Includes index.
 ISBN 1-4027-0727-4
1. Wreaths. I. Gooch, Deon. II. Title.
TT899.75.P63 2004
745.92--dc22

                              2004008961

10 9 8 7 6 5 4 3 2 1

Published by Sterling Publishing Co., Inc.
387 Park Avenue South, New York, NY 10016
©2004 by Pat Poce & Deon Gooch
Distributed in Canada by Sterling Publishing
c/o Manda Group, 165 Dufferin Street
Toronto, Ontario, Canada M6K 3H6
Distributed in Great Britain by Chrysalis Books Group PLC,
The Chrysalis Building, Bramley Road, London W10 6SP, England
Distributed in Australia by Capricorn Link (Australia) Pty. Ltd.
P.O. Box 704, Windsor, NSW 2756, Australia
Printed and Bound in China
All Rights Reserved

Sterling ISBN 1-4027-0727-4

Table of Contents

Section 1:
Basic Wreathmaking
Techniques—14

Section 2:
Beyond the Basic Wreath—36

Section 3:
Wreath Gallery—100

Introduction

A brief history

The first recorded use of wreaths was in ancient Greece where they were used as a head dressing to denote power, position, or accomplishment. They were called diadema or "thing bound around" and they were awarded in the Greek Olympics. At this time, the diadema was made of laurel branches or cloth twisted together to form a simple crown.

At first, the Romans rejected the diadema because raising one person above another was contrary to their belief of democracy. However, it did not take long before the Romans also felt the need to display their power, authority, or prowess through the use of a visible symbol and the diadema once again became an important part of the culture.

Above, two Roman coins picturing Roman Emperors wearing laurel wreaths

Photos by Doug Smith

As the years progressed, precious metals and jewels replaced twigs and leaves as royal crowns. Common people began wearing the traditional laurel branches for holidays or celebrations. Gradually, the laurel branches were replaced with evergreeens, holly, mistletoe, and other foliage as these plants had meaning to the people wearing them.

At some point, wreaths began to be hung on walls and doors, or laid on tables as a decoration. Gradually, the wreath lost its symbolic connection to power or status and is now simply used as a beautiful form of decoration.

Today

Wreaths are used for decoration inside and outside the home. They are not restricted for use only on holidays or celebrations. Some people enjoy celebrating the seasons with theme-oriented wreaths, while others focus on wreath color and texture to complement their interior or exterior decor.

In recent years, wreaths have been made of candy or toys as party favors or with rope, wire, or other objects to complement a decorating theme. Wreaths can be fun as well as beautiful.

It is hoped that this book can help you create wreaths for all your moods and decoration needs. An effort has been made to use a wide variety of materials in the projects featured in this book. It is hoped the reader will learn how to combine and use these items in pleasing and creative ways. Above all, have fun with this book and let your creative imagination flow into new wreath designs.

How to Use This Book

Remember, we all start out at the same point, as newcomers to the art of wreathmaking. You need no special skills or talents; however, a very basic understanding of floral arranging, designing, and floral arranging tools is necessary. The most important requirement is the ability to learn to see how wreaths are constructed. Don't let yourself become frustrated if things do not turn out "perfectly" the first time. The goal of this book is to give you a quick introduction into the basics of wreathmaking and then turn you loose on a variety of projects that get progressively more difficult. There is no better way to learn than from experience. The more wreaths you make, the better you will become at it.

The following pages provide you with a list of the basic tools and materials necessary for wreathmaking. It shows you how to make several key components used to construct a beautiful wreath. It also introduces you to the basic vocabulary of the floral designer.

This book has been divided into three sections. Each project builds upon the skills learned in the previous wreath designs.

Section 1: Basic Wreath-making Techniques

Here you will learn to use some basic techniques to make a series of wreaths. Each project will build upon the skills learned from the previous projects. You will gain experience at manipulating the materials and tools of the wreath maker.

Section 2: Beyond the Basic Wreath

Once you have learned the basic wreathmaking techniques, you are ready to branch out and use those skills in different ways. These projects focus on exploring a variety of different styles and the use of various materials. The reader should gain enough experience that he or she can recognize how any wreath is constructed and thus be able to duplicate the required procedures in designing their own wreaths.

Section 3: Wreath Gallery

This section will show you examples of exceptionally beautiful and creative wreaths. These wreaths transcend craft and enter into the realm of art. These examples of wreathmaking should help you see what kind of work is currently being done in this field and give you some ideas for what you may wish to do.

Above, a 24" fresh pine and seeded eucalyptus Christmas wreath.

How do I get started?

Wreathmaking is simply floral arrangement in a circular fashion. The more you know about where to purchase or gather the materials needed for the arrangement, the easier it will be for you to make attractive wreaths. You would do well to acquaint yourself with local florists and hobby shops. Find people who can answer questions related to floral designs and hobby materials.

Setting up your work space

The first thing you will need is a sturdy craft table. An average-sized kitchen table works fine, but do not use your good furniture because you will be drilling, sawing, cutting, and gluing on this surface. You may wish to cover this table with plastic or even plywood for protection.

Of course, lighting is important. A well-lit work area will allow you to work faster and easier. Remember, the color of a wreath will change slightly when viewed in natural light as opposed to incandescent or florescent lighting.

Place your craft table in a room large enough to lay out your materials for easy access. You should also have a space where you can set your electric glue pan and hot-glue gun, and they will not be tipped or dropped. Of course, you will need several electrical outlets.

If you plan to use spray adhesive, floral spray lacquer, or any other type of spray material, you should ventilate your work area accordingly.

In designing wreaths, it helps to have hooks installed on the wall so the wreath can be hung and visually evaluated. Sometimes the wreath looks entirely different on a wall than on the work table.

A shelf, side table, or cabinet is also helpful to store wreath-building elements for easy access.

You will need a source for water and access to a sink or large tub. For cleaning up, you will need a large garbage can, a broom, and a dustpan.

Safety

Making wreaths is about as safe a hobby as you can find; however, to disregard prudent safety considerations invites injury. Please remember the following safety guidelines:

- Understand and follow manufacturers' instructions regarding the safe operation of all tools and materials.
- Cut away from yourself when using a knife or hacksaw and always hold materials in a secure fashion so they do not slip when cutting.
- Use eye protection when working with power tools or when cutting wire.
- Wear proper attire at all times, remove jewelry and loose clothing, and secure long hair. Wear shoes that will offer adequate protection from falling or sharp objects.
- Make certain hot-glue guns and pan glue are located in secure areas. Pan glue needs to be heated to 360° and may cause severe burns because it can stick to you if spilled.
- Keep your mind on your work. If you can't stay focused on the work, put it away for another day. It is not worth an accident to finish a wreath-making project one day earlier.
- Use common sense at all times.

Basic tools and supplies

As you begin making wreaths, you are going to need a few simple tools and supplies:

Tools
- Florist knife
- Gloves
- Glue gun
- Hacksaw
- Hammer
- Pliers
- Pruning shears
- Safety glasses
- Scissors
- Sink or large tub
- Small electric skillet (for pan glue)
- Small power drill and drill bits
- Tape measure
- Wire cutters

Materials
- Aerosol leaf shine
- Ferning pins
- Floral spray lacquer
- Floral tape: green; brown
- Glue sticks
- Green floral wire: 18 gauge; 21 gauge
- Green wooden floral picks
- Paddle wire
- Pan glue
- Reindeer moss
- Styrofoam (2" thickness)
- Spanish moss

Making your own materials

Most floral arranging materials must be purchased, but there are two commonly used items that you can easily make. These are ferning pins and wrapped floral wire.

Ferning pin

1. Cut a piece from 18-gauge floral wire approximately 3" long.

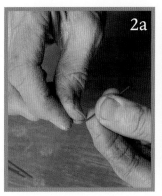

2. Bend the floral wire into a "U" shape to make a perfect ferning pin.

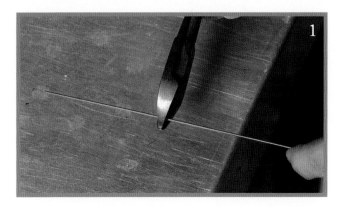

Wrapped floral wire

Floral wire is usually purchased in a green color to blend with green colored foliage. If you are making a wreath using dried foliage or should you are make a wreath using pussy willows, the green wire will stand out and detract from your design. To solve this problem, you can wrap your floral wire with brown floral tape (called "twig" color in some areas of the country).

1. Hold the roll of floral tape in one hand and a length of floral wire in the other. Hold the floral tape taut as you spin the wire and attach the tape to the wire.

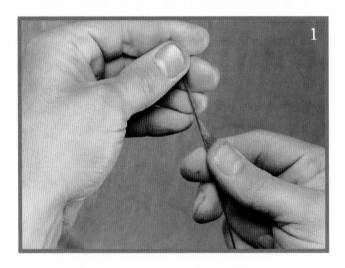

The floral tape will adhere to the wire as it is bent, cut, or twisted. One caution: floral tape can be easily removed from the wire, so avoid handling a tape-covered wire too roughly.

Wreath foliage

Wreaths can be made from a wide variety of materials, but most commonly they are constructed from fresh foliage, dried foliage, or artificial materials made to look like fresh or dried foliage.

Artificial materials have the advantage of lasting an extremely long time without loosing properties such as color, flexibility, or stiffness. Dried foliage lasts a long time, but is often brittle and easily broken. Fresh plants and flowers exhibit unparalleled beauty, but they wilt quickly and many do not dry naturally or very attractively.

While many wreath makers use fresh foliage for arrangements intended to last for only a few days, there is an increasing trend toward fresh wreaths made with foliage which can dry naturally and be kept for an extended period of time. In an effort to help the wreath maker choose appropriate fresh foliage for this type of natural-drying wreath, a partial list of self-drying plants as follows:

- Barley
- Eucalyptus
- Gypsophila (baby's breath)
- Hops
- Hydrangea
- Lavender
- Magnolia
- Oak leaf
- Pepper berry
- Rose
- Salal (lemon leaf)
- Snow berry
- Statice
- Straw flower
- Thistle
- Wheat
- Winter berry
- Yarrow

A floral spray lacquer can enhance the look of fresh foliage and aid in the preservation of the wreath, but it gives the foliage a glossy finish which may not be desired in some instances.

If you reside in a humid climate, you may wish to contact floral designers in your area to see how well fresh plant materials dry in your location.

Hanging a wreath

Some wreath forms come with a mechanism for hanging the wreath when it is finished. For those forms that do not come equipped for hanging, here are a few suggestions.

For a lightweight wreath on a Styrofoam or straw form, apply pan glue on the tips of a ferning pin and insert the pin into the center back portion of the form.

If the wreath will be too heavy to hang by a ferning pin, insert a loop of floral wire through the form before installing the foliage.

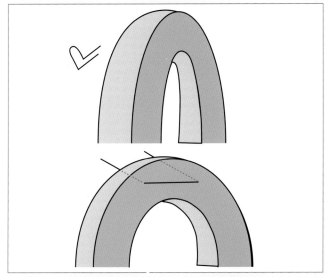

Above top, most wreaths can be hung with a ferning pin. *Above bottom*, insert wire through foam of heavy wreaths.

Some wreaths will not require hangers because the wire form, twigs, or canes of which the wreath is built will serve as a hanger for a nail or hook.

Wire forms are easy to hang because you need only twist the ends of a wire loop around one of the wires on the form. Some wreath makers prefer to install the hanger before actually starting on the wreath because the attachment wires for the wreath can sometimes hinder easy and proper attachment of the hanger.

Cleaning a wreath

This is a major consideration when making a wreath. Naturally, wreaths made of artificial foliage are the easiest to clean because the material is usually more flexible and durable. It can, however, be very time consuming, especially if the wreath has been in a kitchen or bathroom where grease or high humidity trap dirt in the air and deposit it on the wreath.

Most artificial foliage can be cleaned with a soft damp cloth. Gently wipe each leaf or petal to clean off dust and grime.

For the more delicate dried material or fresh flowers which have been allowed to dry naturally, sometimes the only way to clean a wreath is with a can of spray air, or a light feather duster. Hair driers and vacuums can also work if they are not placed on an overly powerful setting.

Some wreath makers refuse to clean a wreath. They simply remove and discard the wreath materials, then reuse the form if possible.

Storing a wreath

One way to prolong the use of a wreath, especially a seasonally oriented wreath is to store it. The best method for storage is to wrap the wreath in tissue paper and place it in a cardboard box. Both the tissue paper and the cardboard box will breath a little and they will also absorb a certain amount of moisture from the wreath.

Wreaths can also be hung on a coat hanger or a wooden rod in a closet. To keep off dust, cover the wreath with paper or an unsealed plastic dry cleaning bag. Storing a wreath in a sealed plastic container or in a tied plastic bag may allow mold to grow on the wreath.

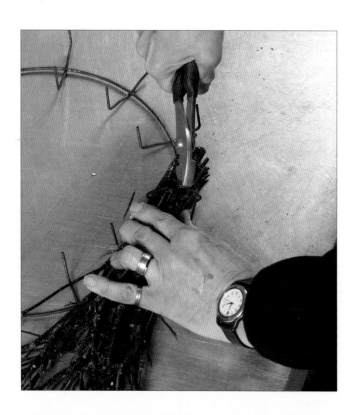

Section 1: Basic Wreathmaking Techniques

1
Technique

What you need to get started:

Tools:
• Basic tools and supplies on page 11

Materials:
• 24" dia. straw form

• Artificial ivy/oak leaves, large (30)

• Artificial ranunculi (75)

• Artificial pink hydrangea blooms (3)

• Floral bird's nest

Expected wreath life:
• Indefinite

How do I use a straw form to make a wreath?

The common premade straw form is easy to use. Floral elements are simply inserted into the straw or glued onto the surface. It is always better if you strengthen the stems of your foliage by adding a floral pick and wrapping with floral tape before inserting into any wreath.

Beginning Floral Wreath

Here's how:

1. Remove packaging from straw form and lay face up on table.

2. Stiffen stems of artificial large ivy/oak leaf by placing a floral pick next to stem and wrapping floral pick and stem together with green floral tape. Stiffen all ivy/oak stems to be used in wreath in this manner.

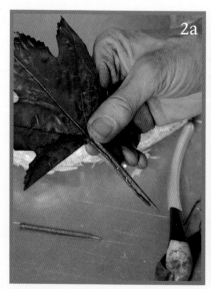

Continued on page 18

Above: finished project size: 24" diameter.

Continued from page 16

3. Insert two rows of ivy/oak leaves into outside edge of straw form.

4. Insert several ivy/oak leaves to form a grouping on the right and left inside edges of straw form.

5. Stiffen stems of flowers with floral picks and floral tape. (Refer to Step 2 on page 16.) Artificial ranunculi were used for this project.

6. Insert ranunculi in small groupings, or bouquets, over most of the remaining form front.

7. Using wire cutters, cut off hydrangea blooms and dip stems in pan glue. Adhere around ranunculi to fill in gaps.

8. Dip bird's nest in pan glue and adhere it among flowers at bottom of wreath.

9. Securely adhere ferning pin into back of straw form to use as a hanger. (Refer to Hanging a wreath on page 13.)

How do I make a grapevine wreath?

Grapevine wreaths look challenging, but they are actually simple to make and decorate. The secret to working with grapevines is to only work with three or four vines at a time and to cut them into manageable sections.

Grapevine Wreath

Here's how:

1. Using pruning shears, cut grapevines into 3'–5' sections. Do not make them exactly the same length.

2. Select three vines and using wire cutters and 21-gauge wire wrapped with brown floral tape, wire vines together. (Refer to Wrapped floral wire on pages 11–12.) Stagger ends so they are not all together.

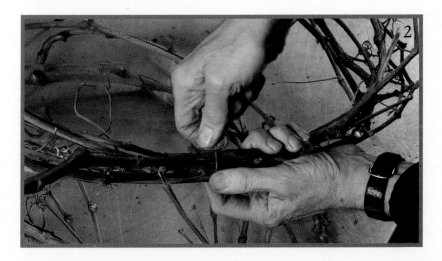

3. Twist vines into a circle. Wherever wreath threatens to come apart, add three more vines, then wire together. Twist new vines around existing vines in wreath. Allow some ends to

2
Technique

What you need to get started:

Tools:
- Basic tools and supplies on page 11

Materials:
- Grapevines (25)
- Fresh magnolia leaves (30)
- Fresh hydrangea blooms (5)

Expected wreath life:
- 6–10 months

Above: finished project size: 36" diameter.

protrude inward and outward so wreath looks natural and not contrived. Continue to add vines until wreath is approximately 3"–4" thick.

4. Using pruning shears, clip fresh magnolia leaves from branch.
   NOTE: Magnolia leaves dry naturally and make perfect foliage for a wreath.

5. Using pan glue, adhere magnolia leaves into five rosetta patterns on grapevine wreath.

6. When glue has dried, spray leaves with floral spray lacquer for a lasting shine.

7. Using pruning shears, clip off hydrangea stems and glue hydrangea blooms onto leaf rosettas.
   NOTE: As with magnolia leaves, hydrangeas will dry naturally.

3
Technique

What you need to get started:

Tools:
• Basic tools and supplies on page 11

Materials:
• 20" dia. clamping form

• Dogwood branches (30)

• Artificial peonies and dahlias, large (25)

Expected wreath life:
• Indefinite

How do I use a clamping form to make a wreath?

Branches can be made into beautiful wreaths with the use of a clamping form. This form not only establishes the size and shape of the wreath, it also provides the perfect structure to attach the various elements of the wreath.

Twig Wreath

Here's how:

1. Using pruning shears, cut dogwood branches so twigs are approximately 18" long and not excessively "brushy."

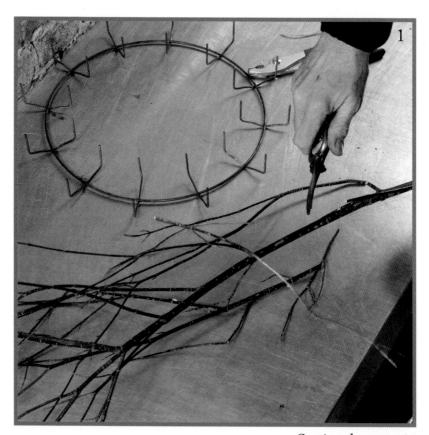

Continued on page 24

Above: finished project size: 40" diameter.

Continued from page 22

2. Select 8–10 twigs and place bottom ends together. Place twig ends on clamping form and using pliers, clamp twigs in place.

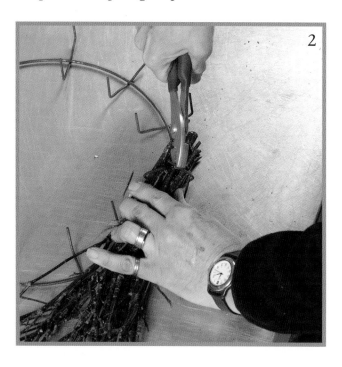

3. Select another 8–10 twigs and place ends in next clamp on clamping form, with loose ends over previously clamped twigs. Repeat clamping process until entire wreath is formed.

4. Using wire cutters, clip stems from artificial flowers, leaving approximately 1½" nub. Dip flower nub in pan glue and adhere over wire clamps. (Refer to photograph on page 23.)

5. Clip and glue leaves from flower stems to fill in around flowers.

How do I use a Styrofoam form to make a wreath?

Styrofoam is a lightweight and stable material for floral forms. Styrofoam forms come in various sizes and shapes.

Styrofoam Wreath

Here's how:

1. Place Styrofoam form on work surface.

2. Using pruning shears, clip salal leaf stems from branches.

What you need to get started:

Tools:
• Basic tools and supplies on page 11

Materials:
• 14" sq. Styrofoam form
• Fresh salal branches (18)
• Dried lotus pods (11)
• Seeded Styrofoam balls (36)

Expected wreath life:
• Indefinite

Above: finished project size: 17" square.

3. Evenly space and pin salal leaves on back side of Styrofoam form, with leaves facing toward inside and outside edges.

4. Using wire cutters, cut 3" piece of 18-gauge wire. Dip one end into pan glue, then push glued wire into seeded ball.

5. Turn form over. Dip wire on seeded ball into pan glue and insert seeded balls into Styrofoam form around the inside and outside edges.

6. Install ferning pin hanger before front of wreath is covered with foliage. (Refer to Hanging a wreath page 13.)

7. Trim lotus pod stems to 1½".

8. Dip lotus pod stems in pan glue, then insert stems uniformly spaced around face of Styrofoam form.

9. Fill in empty spaces around seeded balls and lotus pods with reindeer moss. Attach moss with ferning pins.

10. Finish wreath by gluing seeded balls in areas needing an extra touch.

NOTES: When making a wreath, there is always more space to fill than expected. Lichens, moss, dried plants and flowers, or even artificial foliage can be glued or pinned in to fill in empty spots on the wreath.

To help preserve a wreath, seal it with floral spray lacquer. This is sometimes called floral glaze or spray sealant. This material will put a shine on the wreath, so avoid using it if your wreath needs a matte finish.

How do I make a simple tied wreath?

Pussy willows are perfect to bend and shape into a simple tied wreath; but plan on making this wreath between February and March because pussy willow blooms are very seasonal.

Pussy Willow Wreath

Here's how:

1. Form a four-sided wreath with pussy willow stems approximately 24" long. Each side should have 3–5 stems. (Refer to photograph on page 30.) Place horizontal stems on work table and vertical stems on top. Stagger ends.

2. Tie stems together at the corners with twine. Make a crisscross lashing with the knot on top.

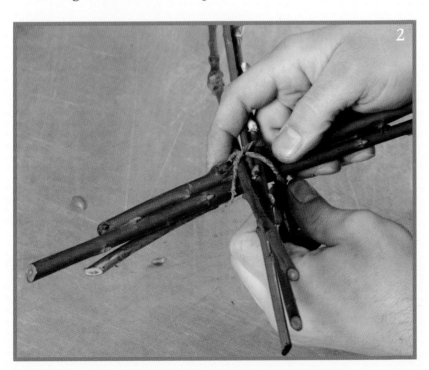

What you need to get started:

Tools:
• Basic tools and supplies on page 11

Materials:
• Pussy willow stems (25)
• Jute twine, heavy duty
• Fresh blooming branches (3)
• Dried sponge mushrooms (2)
• Dried monkey pod
• Fresh hydrangea bloom
• Dried protea bloom

Expected wreath life:
• 8–10 months

Above: finished project size: 20" x 30".

3. Using pruning shears, trim ends of stems at an angle. This will add more interest to the wreath.

4. Turn wreath over so twine knots are fastened in back of wreath.

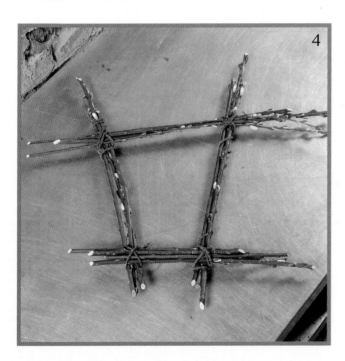

5. Group 6–8 pussy willows or other blooming branches and tie on left arm of wreath. Allow stems to extend unevenly below wreath and well above top of wreath. Splay branches above wreath to form an interesting design.

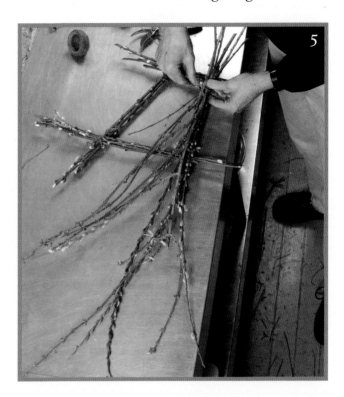

6. Dip two large sponge mushrooms into pan glue and adhere to each side of lashing for blooming branches.

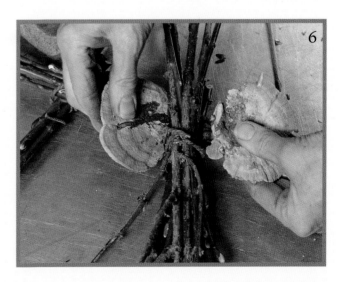

7. Using hacksaw, cut bottom from monkey pod to make accent for mushroom grouping.

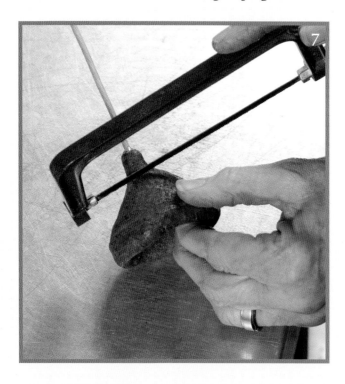

8. Using pan glue, securely adhere monkey pod to mushrooms.

9. Glue in hydrangea and protea blooms to add interest and texture to grouping.

10. Glue some reindeer moss into grouping and on at least one arm of wreath.
   NOTE: The fresh elements of this wreath will dry naturally.

How do I use a wire form to make a wreath?

Flat wire forms are used when many items must be wired together to form the wreath. A wire form is very easy to hang because the wire will hook on almost any nail or hanger. They also make the perfect form if you want to make a two-sided wreath.

Wire Ring Wreath

Here's how:

1. Using pruning shears, clip salal so there are several leaves on each sprig. Attach salal sprigs to wire form with paddle wire. Cover front of form with salal leaves facing both inside and outside edges.

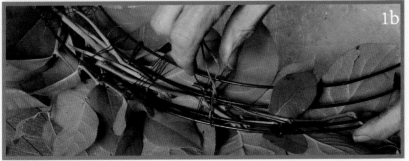

What you need to get started:

Tools:
- Basic tools and supplies on page 11

Materials:
- 14" dia. wire form
- Fresh salal (20)
- Fresh spiral eucalyptus sprigs (10)
- Fresh seeded eucalyptus sprigs (5)
- Fresh hypernicum berry sprigs (10)
- Dried pomegranates (5)

Expected wreath life:
- 8–10 months

Above: finished project size: 22" diameter.

2. Using floral wire, attach spiral eucalyptus sprigs on wreath to create two large floral groupings. (Refer to photograph on page 34.)

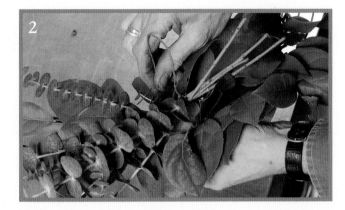

3. Clip sprigs of seeded eucalyptus to layer in front of spiral eucalyptus.

4. Using paddle wire, attach seeded eucalyptus to floral groupings.

5. Wire on hypernicum berry sprigs for color and contrast.

6. Finish wreath by dipping pomegranates in pan glue and adhering them in strategic places around wreath.

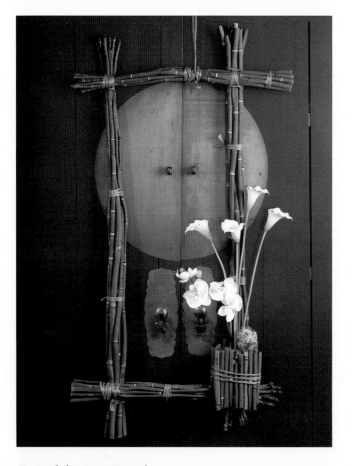

Section 2: Beyond the Basic Wreath

1
Project

How do I make a small vertical festoon?

What you need to get started:

Tools:
• Basic tools and supplies on page 11

Materials:
• 1" dia. bamboo (12')
• Jute twine, heavy duty
• Artificial orchid with roots

Expected wreath life:
• Indefinite

Wreaths need not always be circular. A vertical festoon can fill an awkward space. Fat sticks of bamboo are a good choice when you are going for a vertical look. Simply tie varying lengths of bamboo together with twine and embellish with desired florals.

Vertical Wall Festoon

Here's how:

1. Determine length of festoon by measuring area in which wreath will be located. Using hacksaw, cut bamboo sticks on an angle into five different lengths.

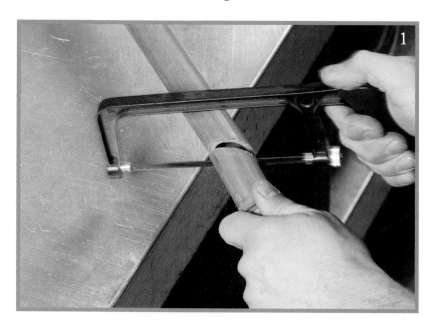

2. Tie twine to one stick and make a knot.

Continued on page 40

Above: finished project size: 34" tall.

Continued from page 38

3. Place bamboo sticks together with ends at varying heights. Wind twine over and under sticks and tighten to hold bamboo together securely.

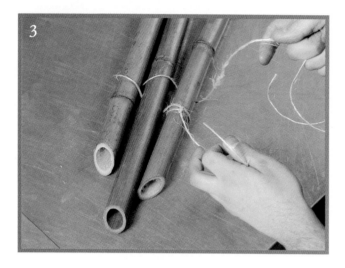

4. When bamboo is secure, wrap twine around the sticks to make a decorative lashing. One long lashing will tie all the sticks together at the top of the festoon. (Refer to photograph on page 39.)

5. It is best if knots are located on the back of the festoon. If knot is on the front, ends must be tucked in and care must be taken to cover the knot with florals.

6. Position artificial orchid along length of vertical bamboo festoon.

7. Using twine, lash the orchid stem in two places along one bamboo stick.

8. Orchid may be tied at the top or secured between two sticks of bamboo.

9. Insert reindeer moss in root area of orchid.

10. Place some reindeer moss into one or two hollow ends of the bamboo.

11. Using drill and ¼" drill bit, bore hole in one piece of bamboo near the top and insert twine. Floral pick may be used to retrieve twine so a knot may be tied in twine and used to hang vertical festoon.

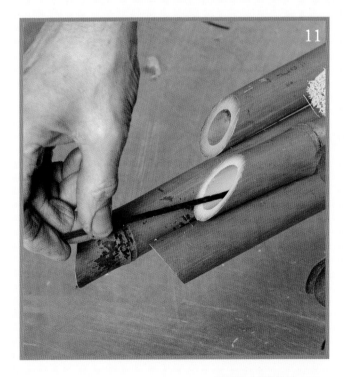

2
Project

What you need to get started:

Tools:
- Basic tools and supplies on page 11

Materials:
- 18" dia. premade artificial ivory-colored berry wreath
- Resin photo frames (2)
- Rattle
- Plush animal
- Baby ribbon (1 yard)

Expected wreath life:
- Indefinite

How do I embellish a purchased wreath?

By adding your own touches to a store-bought wreath, you can create a unique gift with very little effort. Make certain to wire the embellishments onto the wreath securely, and take care not to choose items that are too heavy.

Purchased Wreath

Here's how:

1. Install baby's pictures in resin photo frames.

2. Using brown-taped floral wire, secure frames onto wreath. (Refer to Wrapped floral wire on pages 11–12.)

3. Using brown-taped floral wire, attach rattle and plush animal to wreath.

4. Using scissors, cut baby ribbon in half. Tie baby ribbon around rattle and plush animal.

NOTES: If this wreath is intended for a child's room, make certain all elements on the wreath are firmly attached. Also, insure that wreath is hung high enough so child cannot pull it down and put items into his/her mouth.

Since the baby's pictures are displayed in the resin frames, this wreath would be a perfect gift for a grandparent.

Many items can be used on baby wreaths. Baby booties, bibs, ribbons, toys, pacifiers, or any other baby-related items. These wreaths can be used as centerpieces for baby showers or birthday parties.

Above: finished project size: 18" diameter.

3

Project

What you need to get started:

Tools:
- Basic tools and supplies on page 11

Materials:
- 20" dia. wet foam form
- Fresh salal branches (20)
- Aerosol leaf shine
- Seeded eucalyptus sprigs (6)
- Fresh Italian ruscus sprigs (20)
- Fresh baby's breath sprigs (12)
- Fresh Sahara Roses (50)
- Fresh green hypernicum berry sprigs (10)
- Fresh blue hydrangea blooms (3)

Expected wreath life:
- 8–10 months

How do I make a fresh wreath?

When prepared properly, a fresh wreath may be enjoyed for several days. Use a wet foam form and saturate completely with water before adding the fresh florals. By selecting florals that dry nicely, you can enhance the life of your wreath for many months to come.

Elegant Fresh Wreath

Here's how:

1. Fill tub with water and place wet foam form face down in tub. Allow form to soak up water for approximately 15 minutes. Remove and place face up on work table.

2. Using pruning shears, cut salal so there are 2–3 leaves per sprig, leaving stem long enough to insert into wet foam form. Insert two rows each of salal leaves on inside and outside of form.

Continued on page 46

Above: finished project size: 22" diameter.

Continued from page 44

3. Spray salal leaves liberally with aerosol leaf shine. Allow leaves to dry.

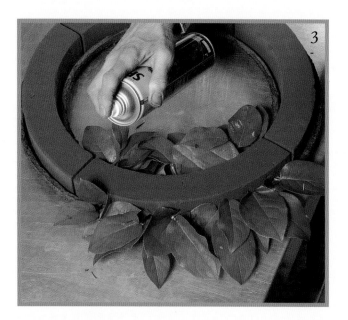

4. Clip sprigs of seeded eucalyptus and insert over salal leaves on both inside and outside edges of wreath.

5. Insert sprigs of Italian ruscus along front of form. Once inserted, sprigs should lay flat and cover form.

6. Clip sprigs of baby's breath and insert in and around Italian ruscus and next to seeded eucalyptus.

7. Prune Sahara Roses to leave a 2" stem and insert over entire wreath.

8. Clip sprigs of green hypernicum to nestle next to rose blossoms to give texture and volume to wreath.

9. Clip sections from blue hydrangeas, leaving enough stem to insert into wreath form.

10. Insert hydrangea clippings into form between Sahara Roses to add color.

4

Project

What you need to get started:

Tools:
- Basic tools and supplies on page 11

Materials:
- 24" dia. premade dried eucalyptus wreath
- Craft store fishing decorations

Expected wreath life:
- 8–10 months

How do I make a theme wreath?

Wreaths are an excellent way to enhance a room scheme. Try using sports paraphernalia for your little soccer player's room, dragonflies and butterflies add to a garden theme, or make a delightful gift for the fisherman on your Christmas list. Craft stores have a large variety of "themed" decorations, or use your own collection of memorabilia to give the wreath a more personal touch.

Fishing Wreath

Here's how:

1. Glue two ferning pins into the back of the wreath and string paddle wire between ferning pins.

2. Using green-taped floral wire, secure large fishing pole onto wreath at top and bottom of pole.
   NOTE: Use floral wire covered with green floral tape rather than bare floral wire because taped wire clings tighter to the items being wired into the wreath.

3. Using either pan glue or a hot-glue gun, adhere fishing decorations onto wreath.

   Notes: Artificial flowers or tole-painted objects may also be glued or wired into wreath to tie the wreath into the color scheme of your room.
   This is an especially good project to use as a gift.

Above: finished project size: 24" diameter.

5

Project

What you need to get started:

Tools:
- Basic tools and supplies on page 11

Materials:
- Heart-shaped twig form
- Gold floral foil
- Floral foam block (1)
- Charlotte Roses (25)

Expected wreath life:
- 6–10 months

How do I use a premade specialty form?

Sometimes wreath forms come in shapes that you cannot easily make yourself, such as this heart-shaped twig wreath. Select a wreath that is fairly deep so that the flowers fit snugly inside. Moss helps to fill in the gaps and define the lines of your design.

Valentine Wreath

Here's how:

1. Using scissors, cut a square of florist foil more than twice the size needed to line center of form. Fold foil in half for more strength.

Continued on page 52

Above: finished project size: 10" x 14".

Continued from page 50

2. Mold florist foil to fit inside cavity of form.

3. Cut or fold excess foil so it becomes level with top of form.

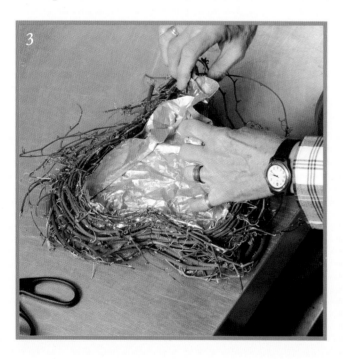

4. Fill sink or tub with water to soak floral foam. Using florist knife, slice off 1"–1½" sections. Only soak enough foam to fill form cavity.

5. Break or cut floral foam to fit into foil-lined cavity of form.

6. Using pruning shears, cut rose stems to 1". Clip stems at an angle for inserting into foam.

7. Insert roses around inside edge of form, fitting blooms closely so floral foam does not show through.

8. Fill in center of heart-shaped form with closely fitting blooms.

9. Use knife to push in reindeer moss around outer edge of the roses to create textured edging for flowers and to conceal foil.

6

Project

What you need to get started:

Tools:
- Basic tools and supplies on page 11

Materials:
- 24" dia. premade artificial fern, ivy, and berry form
- Plush bunny
- Easter egg garland
- Artificial lavender hydrangea blooms (6)
- Artificial purple pansies (7)
- Artificial pink azalea blooms (10)

Expected wreath life:
- Indefinite

How do I make a seasonal wreath?

By choosing flowers appropriate for each season, you can change the look of your wreath several times within the season. For example, this Spring wreath looks great on its own; but when Easter comes along, a cute bunny and a string of egg garland can be easily added. For Mother's Day, you may want to add some gardening embellishments.

Seasonal Wreath

Here's how:

1. Wire plush bunny into top of wreath with green-taped floral wire. (Refer to Wrapped floral wire on pages 11–12.)

2. Using hot-glue gun, adhere Easter egg garland into wreath.

3. Using wire cutters, clip hydrangea stems to 1½", then dip stems in pan glue and adhere onto wreath.

4. Clip the stems on pansies and glue into wreath to complement the hydrangeas.

5. Clip the stems on azaleas and glue into wreath, filling in any empty spaces.

6. If premade wreath does not have a hanger, glue in ferning pin hanger or attach floral wire hanger. (Refer to Hanging a wreath on page 13.)

Above: finished project size: 24" diameter.

7 Project

What you need to get started:

Tools:
- Basic tools and supplies on page 11

Materials:
- 36" river cane sticks (15)
- Jute twine, heavy duty
- Artificial orchids with roots (2)
- Mossed Styrofoam balls (4)

Expected wreath life:
- Indefinite

How can I make a wreath using river cane?

A nontraditional square wreath can be easily made using river cane sticks. These sturdy sticks are tied at the corners with twine. Beautiful silk orchids finish off the design for a simple, yet elegant look.

River Cane Wreath

Here's how:

1. Using florist knife, cut river cane on an angle roughly in half.

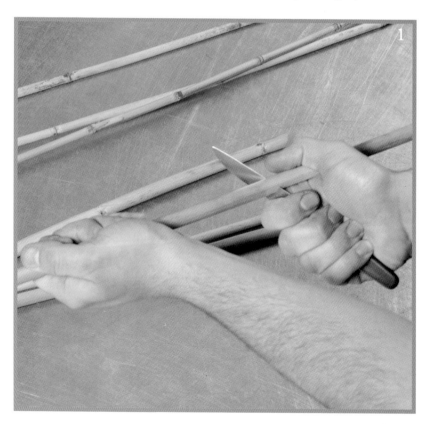

Continued on page 58

Above: finished project size: 22" square.

Continued from page 56

2. Set three slender canes aside. Place four sets of five canes together, staggering ends, and tie at each end with twine.

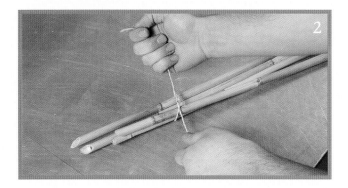

3. Lay two horizontal bundles of cane on table with two vertical bundles on top. Lash corners together with knots being tied on back of wreath. (Refer to How do I make a simple tied wreath, Steps 1-4 on pages 29–31.)

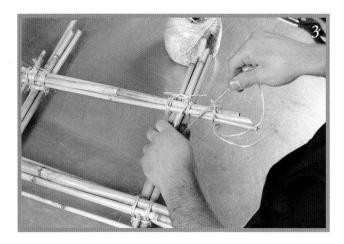

4. Install wire hanger. (Refer to Hanging a wreath page 13.)

5. Turn wreath right side up. Tie one of the slender canes approximately 1" away from the main bundle on the right of the wreath. Tie another slender cane 1" under the bottom horizontal bundle.

6. Using power drill and ¼" bit, drill a hole in bottom-left corner of the wreath.

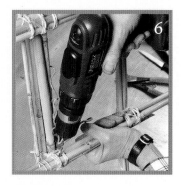

7. Using knife, trim roots of both orchids so they fit in drilled hole. Dip both orchid roots in pan glue and insert into hole.

8. Make one orchid stand straight up and bend the other so it angles over the center of the wreath.

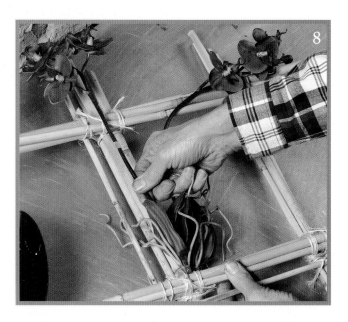

9. Pin Spanish moss over root area of orchids with ferning pins.

10. Clip wires from three mossed balls, dip balls in pan glue, and adhere over spanish moss.

11. Drill hole through remaining mossed ball and insert one slender river cane through hole.

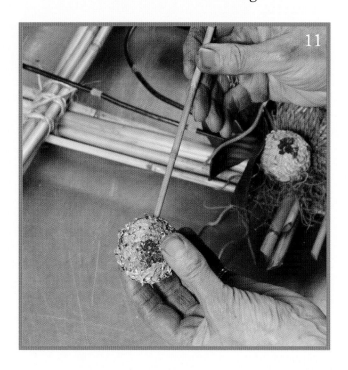

12. Tie mossed ball and river cane at the top-right corner of wreath.

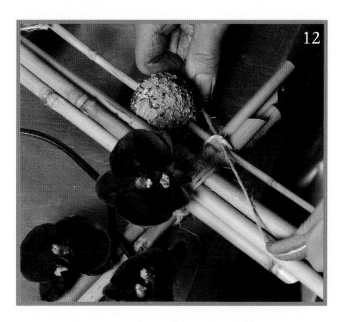

12. Slant cane downward and tie remaining end of cane to left side of wreath.

8

Project

What you need to get started:

Tools:
- Basic tools and supplies on page 11

Materials:
- 16" sq. wire form
- Fresh lavender sprigs (12 large bunches)
- Green sheer wire-edged ribbon (3 yards)

Expected wreath life:
- 6–10 months

How do I make an aromatic lavender wreath?

The beauty of this wreath is that it is quick and easy to make, and it smells delightful. Once the aroma of the lavender has faded, simply pull off some of the old blooms and insert some new sprigs. For a more intense scent, a little bit of lavender oil can be added to some of the sprigs. Lavender is known for its calming effect, so this wreath would be perfect in a bath area or in the bedroom.

Lavender Wreath

Here's how:

1. Using green-taped floral wire, tie three bunches of lavender onto each side of square wire form. (Refer to Wrapped floral wire on pages 11–12.) Hide wire by overlapping lavender bunches. (Refer to Wire Ring Wreath on pages 33–35.)

2. Using scissors, cut ribbon into one yard lengths.

3. Tie two ribbons in decorative bows on upper-left and lower-right sections of wreath.

4. Tie ends of remaining ribbon in two places at top of wreath frame for hanging.

   NOTE: This same technique can be used with fresh wheat, strawflowers, barley, or hops. It can also be done with dried material such as star flowers, hill flowers, or any other dried flower that can be grouped and tied.

Above: finished project size: 16" square.

Project 9

How do I make a whorl-shaped wreath?

A whorl-shaped wreath can be made by wiring twigs onto a round wire form. Fresh pussy willows are used in this application because they continue to flower.

Pussy Willow Whorl

What you need to get started:

Tools:
- Basic tools and supplies on page 11

Materials:
- 24" dia. two-strand wire form
- Fresh pussy willow stems (80)

Expected wreath life:
- 1–2 years

Here's how:

1. Using wire cutters, cut 45 12" sections of 21-gauge floral wire. Wrap each wire with brown floral tape. (Refer to Wrapped floral wire on pages 11–12.)

2. Select five 2½' pussy willow stems and wire them to the wire form approximately half way up the stems.
   NOTE: Wreath will look more natural if tips of the pussy willows are staggered.

Continued on page 64

Above: finished project size: 36" diameter.

Continued from page 62

3. Go down about 4"–6" and wire the stems to the form again.

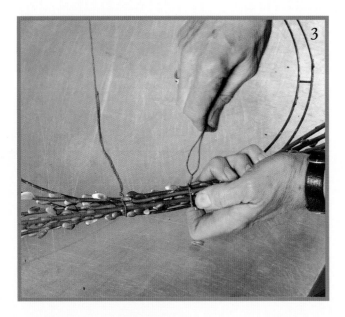

4. Using pruning shears, trim bottom of pussy willow stems unevenly so they will lay flatter on the wreath and wire them to the form.

5. Using wire cutters, cut off wire ends.

6. Create another five-branch bundle and wire further along form so pussy willow tips splay outward in a pleasing fashion. On occasion, you may have to unwire the pussy willow bundle and reposition the branches to make them work properly.

7. Continue to add pussy willow bundles until the wreath is complete (approximately 15–16 sections).

   NOTE: A larger pussy willow wreath can be made if a six-wire form is used. Try to keep the pussy willow bundles as flat as possible so the form is covered but the pussy willow branches do not overpower the form and make an excessively heavy wreath.

How can I make a corner wreath for my door, window, or picture frame?

As corner wreaths, or sprays, are becoming more popular, forms and materials are being offered to make this specialized decoration. In this project, a floral cage form is used to enable you to add materials both vertically and horizontally.

Corner Wreath

Here's how:

1. Arrange long stiff-stemmed ivy along two edges of cage form to establish a horizontal and vertical arm for wreath.

What you need to get started:

Tools:
- Basic tools and supplies on page 11

Materials:
- Floral cage form
- Artificial ivy stems: plain; variegated
- Artificial eucalyptus sprigs
- Artificial corkscrew willow stems
- Artificial hypernicum berry sprigs

Expected wreath life:
- Indefinite

Above: finished project size: 30" x 28".

2. Fill in around form with eucalyptus and ivy sprigs. Use both plain and variegated ivy stems.

3. Include corkscrew willow stems for texture.

4. Add hypernicum berry sprigs for color and accent.

   NOTE: You may wish to add some flowers of your choosing in addition to the foliage specified in the project.

NOTES: This wreath ornament can be used on the corner of a picture, a mirror, a hutch, a window, a fireplace mantel, or a doorway. It can be used on a wall as part of a grouping that may include pictures, lamps, wall ornaments, or antiques. It is perfect for a living room, hall, bedroom, or kitchen.

Some floral designers use a pair of these corner wreaths to create an arbor effect over a doorway or on a fireplace mantel.

11
Project

What you need to get started:

Tools:
• Basic tools and supplies on page 11

Materials:
• Floral foil
• Grapevines (30)
• Small clay pots (7–10)
• Floral bird's nests (2)
• Small potted plants (7–10)
• Dried quince sections

Expected wreath life:
• Indefinite

How can I make a wreath to hang outside?

A wreath containing live plants is perfect to hang on an outside fence, shed, or in the garden. This particular wreath can be changed and replenished as the season progresses. Don't forget to water your wreath often, especially when it is placed in an area that receives full sun.

Outside Wreath

Here's how:

1. Begin by making a 30" dia. grapevine wreath. (Refer to Grapevine Wreath, Steps 1–3 on pages 19–21.)

2. Use a clay pot to mold a double layer of florist foil into water-proof liners for the small clay pots which will eventually be fastened into wreath. Set liners aside.

Continued on page 70

Above: finished project size: 30" diameter.

Continued from page 68

3. Using wire cutters, cut floral picks into 2"–2½" sections and glue them into an "X" shape. Place glued floral picks in bottom of small clay pots.

4. Tie crossed floral pick into bottom of pot with 10" of 18-gauge wire wrapped with brown floral tape and hot glued in place. (Refer to Wrapped floral wire on pages 11–12.)

5. Use wire ends to tie pots into wreath. Tie some pots in groups and others individually. Arrange pots so they are generally pointing upward.

6. Spiral-wrap wreath and pots with grapevines to add interest and give a "circular motion" to the wreath.

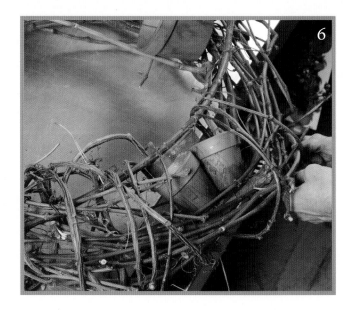

7. Insert foil liners into each clay pot on wreath.

8. Glue floral bird's nests into wreath or clay pots. Plant appropriate seasonal plants into pots to give wreath color and soft floral texture.

9. Water plants and hang wreath outdoors. As flowers outgrow the pots, or as the season changes, replace plants more appropriate for the season.

10. For a little extra color and texture, glue in some dried quince sections and a little reindeer moss around the wreath. (Refer to photograph on page 69.)

NOTE: At the end of the growing season, the live plants can be replaced with artificial foliage and the wreath can then be taken indoors to enjoy for the winter.

12 Project

What you need to get started:

Tools:
- Basic tools and supplies on page 11
- Circular saw
- Screwdriver

Materials:
- Plywood (¼" x 22" x 14")
- Spray paint, matte black
- 8" floral papier-mâché cones (3)
- Latex paint, taupe
- D-rings and mounting screws (2 sets)
- Metal hanger rod (24")
- Decorative finials (2)
- French wired-edged ribbon (1 yard)
- Dried wheat, flowers, and lavender

Expected wreath life:
- Indefinite

How can I make a floral wall hanging?

This wall hanging is very unique and versatile. Different looks can be easily achieved by replacing the dried florals in the cones. Try using all white florals for a chic country look, or decorate for the holidays by choosing seasonal foliage.

Floral Wall Display

Here's how:

1. Using a circular saw, cut plywood into proper dimensions.

2. Spray-paint the plywood with matte black.

3. Slightly mash floral papier-mâché cones so openings are oblong. Dip cones into latex paint so they are heavily coated with paint. Allow to dry for 48 hours.

4. Using screwdriver mount D-rings on back of plywood with curve of metal "D" facing up.

5. Using hot-glue gun or pan glue, adhere painted cones to plywood with cone points touching bottom of plywood.

6. Assemble metal hanger rod and finials.

7. Using scissors, cut ribbon in half. Thread one length through D-ring and tie in a bow to metal hanger rod.

8. Insert dried wheat, an assortment of dried flowers, and dried lavender into cones.

Above: finished project size: 22" x 14".

13

Project

What you need to get started:

Tools:
- Basic tools and supplies on page 11

Materials:
- 20" dia. premade twig wreath
- Fall pumpkin garland
- Tole-painted pumpkins (5)

Expected wreath life:
- Indefinite

How can I make a wreath using a purchased garland?

There are many wonderful garland choices on the market. Wrapping a garland throughout a wreath makes a more dramatic statement than you would get if you just decorated with a simple strand of the garland itself. For an added touch, this wreath was embellished with painted wooden cutouts.

Garland Wreath

Here's how:

1. Either purchase or make a 22" twig wreath. (Refer to Grapevine Wreath, Steps 1–3 on pages 19–21.)

2. Using a brown-taped wire, attach a 6' fall pumpkin garland into wreath. (Refer to Wrapped floral wire on pages 11–12.)
   NOTE: Most garlands come in 9' lengths, but this wreath only needs 6'.

3. Using pan glue or a hot-glue gun, adhere five tole-painted pumpkins to wreath.

   NOTES: Either by selecting a different garland or by choosing specialized items for the wreath, you can make a decoration especially for Thanksgiving or Halloween.

   Use this same basic wreath idea for other holidays or seasons. Craft stores carry seasonal garlands and accents for most universally celebrated events.

Above: finished project size: 20" diameter.

What different materials can I use to make a wreath?

What you need to get started:

Tools:
- Basic tools and supplies on page 11

Materials:
- Snake grass stems (50–60)
- Rubber bands (8)
- Raffia
- Styrofoam 2½" x 4" x 1½"
- Artificial orchids (5)
- Mossed Styrofoam ball

Expected wreath life:
- Indefinite

There are many types of plants such as snake grass that may be used to make a wreath. The key is to find those that dry naturally.

Snake Grass Wreath

Here's how:

1. Group 12–15 snake grass stems and secure cut ends with rubber band. Repeat with bud ends. Beginning at cut end, tie snake grass bundle together with raffia every 10".

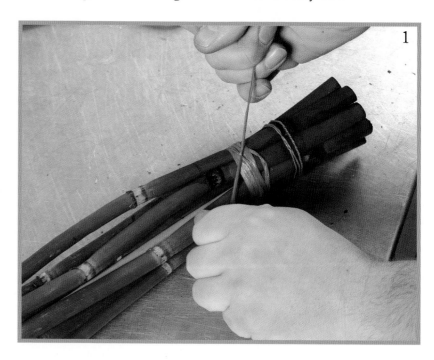

2. Using raffia, tie four bunches of snake grass stems. Cut away rubber bands after bundles are tied.

Continued on page 78

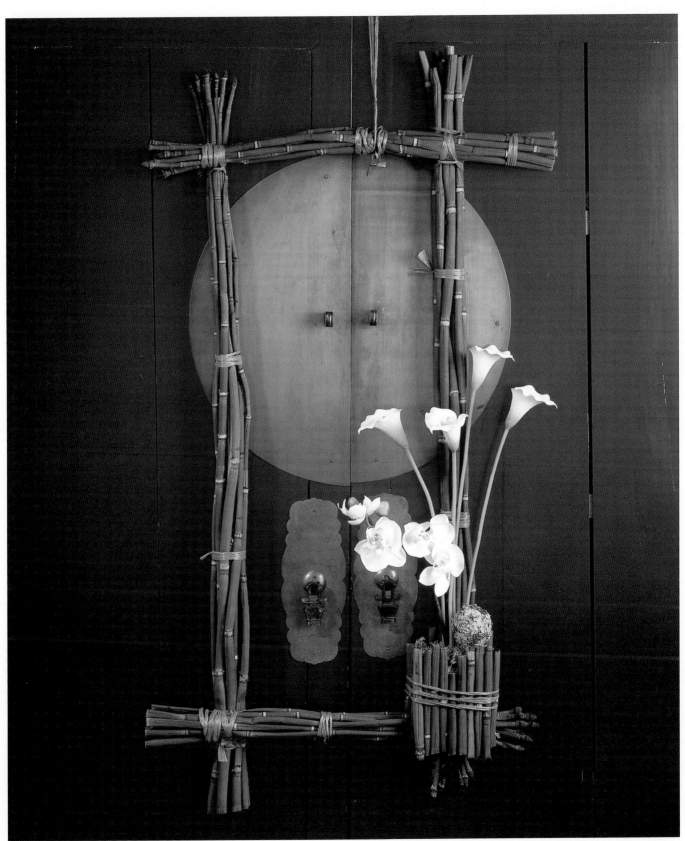

Above: finished project size: 20" x 36".

Continued from page 76

3. Cut two bundles in half to make short ends of wreath (one bundle cut in half will not work because two sets of bud ends are needed).

4. Arrange long bundles of snake grass so one bundle has bud ends pointing up and the other has bud ends facing down. Take short bundles of snake grass and lay them across long bundles with bud ends of short bundles matching up with bud ends of long bundles. Lash bundles together with raffia to form a rectangle.

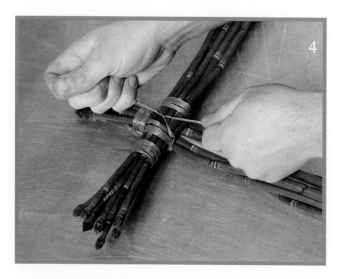

5. Glue Styrofoam block onto bottom-right corner of the wreath and tie in place to help glue set properly.

6. Clip unused snake grass stems to 4" lengths and glue onto Styrofoam block to form a box.

7. Tie snake grass box with raffia for decorative effect.

8. Insert arrangement of artificial orchids into Styrofoam block, then cover the block with reindeer moss.

9. Finish wreath by adding a mossed Styrofoam ball as an accent.

10. Hang wreath by tying raffia loop to top bundle of snake grass.

NOTES: If roses were substituted for the orchids, the character of the wreath would change to a Victorian look. Of course, placement of the wreath in the home would have a great deal to do with how the style of the wreath was interpreted.

Take the same wreath and add only greenery for decoration and the wreath would give the general feeling of a European garden.

15
Project

What you need to get started:

Tools:
- Basic tools and supplies on page 11

Materials:
- 36" dia. grapevine wreath
- Artificial ivy stems (12)
- Artificial corkscrew willow stems (12)
- Artificial forsythia branches (6)
- Artificial tulips (36)
- Artificial hyacinth blooms (12)
- Artificial daffodils (24)
- Artificial aster stems (12)

Expected wreath life:
- Indefinite

There are no hard and fast rules for wreath design. Pick colors that work well together and florals of varying sizes and textures. Arrange them into your wreath prior to gluing them, so that if something is not quite working, you can change it.

Early Spring Wreath

Here's how:

1. Either purchase or make a 36" dia. grapevine wreath. (Refer to Grapevine Wreath, Steps 1–3 on pages 19–21.)

2. Using pan glue, adhere ivy, corkscrew willow stems, and forsythia branches around entire front of wreath.

3. Using wire cutters, trim stems off tulips, hyacinth blooms, daffodils, and aster sprigs so they may be glued into wreath.

4. Using pan glue, attach blooms into wreath so grapevine understructure is covered.
   NOTE: Some people prefer a simple wreath. Others will expand the wreath. This is a perfect project to use floral odds and ends that accumulate in most floral designers' work rooms.

5. Because this wreath is so large and heavy, install a strong wire hanger to the back of the wreath. (Refer to Hanging a wreath on page 13.)

Above: finished project size: 40" diameter.

16 Project

How can I make a rustic wreath using rope and other western elements?

What you need to get started:

Tools:
- Basic tools and supplies on page 11

Materials:
- 20" dia. wire form
- 1" dia. natural hemp rope with whipped ends (25')
- Jute twine, heavy duty
- Rusty barbed wire
- Rusty horseshoes (5)
- Spur
- Rusty stars
- Mushroom pods (6)

Expected wreath life:
- Indefinite

A coil of rope is a perfect base for this western wreath. Because the rope is quite heavy, make certain to use heavy-duty twine when attaching the rope to the wire wreath form. Rusty stars, horseshoes, and spurs are perfect embellishments and are also securely attached with the twine.

Western Wreath

Here's how:

1. Place form on work table. Make certain that cutting tools are appropriate for heavy materials.

Continued on page 84

Above: finished project size: 24" x 30".

Continued from page 82

2. Coil rope over wire form, leaving about 5' of rope on bottom to make rope "bow."

3. Tie rope to wire form in four locations with heavy-duty twine.

4. Form rope "bow" at bottom of wreath and tie to rope coil with twine.

5. Loop barbed wire around rope, then lash rope, wire, and wire ring together with twine. You may wish to use gloves.

6. Lash horseshoes and spur to various areas on the wreath.

7. Tie secure knot in top loop of each rusty star.

8. Push rusty stars into rope coil and tie in place. *NOTE*: If you can not find rusty stars, any type of rusty item will work. Of course, you will need to find an antique-looking item that relates to cowboys or horses.

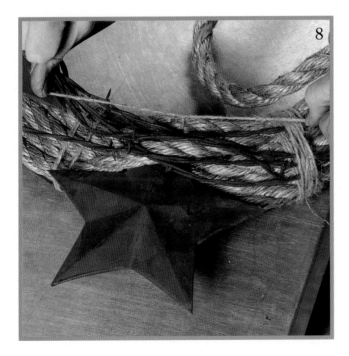

9. Clip off attachment wires on mushroom pods.

10. Glue the mushroom pods into rope "bow" for finishing touch.

Project 17

Project

What you need to get started:

Tools:
- Basic tools and supplies on page 11

Materials:
- 30" dia. clamping form
- Corkscrew willow stems (30)
- Artificial laurel leaf branches (6)
- Artificial seeded eucalyptus stems (8)
- Artificial mimosa foliage stems (3)
- Artificial kale (2)
- Artificial ivory-colored lilies (3)
- Artificial ivory-colored open roses (3)

Expected wreath life:
- Indefinite

How do I make a wreath from corkscrew willow?

Making twig wreaths looks difficult, but it is really easy provided you choose the proper clamping form. Small forms are used with supple twigs, but brittle twigs are best used with large forms that do not require tight bends.

Corkscrew Willow Wreath

Here's how:

1. Clamp corkscrew willow stems into clamping form. (Refer to Twig Wreath, Steps 1–3 on pages 22–24.)

2. Using pan glue, adhere laurel leaf branches to center of wreath to cover clamping form.

3. Glue eucalyptus sprigs so they extend outward into the corkscrew willow stems.

4. Glue mimosa foliage to fill in and add body to wreath.

5. Using wire cutters, trim stems from lilies and roses so they can be glued into wreath.

6. Glue kale, lilies, and roses into groupings on wreath.

7. Either hang wreath from clamping form or attach wire hanger. (Refer to Hanging a wreath on page 13.)

Above: finished project size: 32" diameter.

18 Project

What you need to get started:

Tools:
- Basic tools and supplies on page 11

Materials:
- 1" dia. bamboo sticks, 12'
- Jute twine, heavy duty
- 4" sq. x 2" Styrofoam block
- Artificial ivory- burgundy-colored cherry blossom stems
- Large resin leaves (3)
- Artificial green hypernicum berry sprig
- Twine ball

Expected wreath life:
- Indefinite

How do I attach a wreath to a substantial base, such as thick bamboo??

By drilling small holes into the base and gluing floral picks into the holes, you create a sturdy holder for a Styrofoam block.

Oriental Bamboo Wreath

Here's how:

1. Using hacksaw, cut bamboo sticks in 3' sections.

2. Lash sticks together with twine to form a bamboo square. (Refer to River Cane Wreath, Steps 2–3 on page 58.)

Continued on page 90

Above: finished project size: 24" square.

Continued from page 88

3. Using power drill, bore two ³⁄₁₆" holes in the upper-left section of wreath approximately 4" apart. Glue two floral picks into the holes. Allow glue to dry for 15 minutes.

4. Press floral picks through Styrofoam block so top of block rests firmly against the horizontal bamboo stick.

5. Remove Styrofoam block from floral picks and apply pan glue where block will come in contact with the stick.

6. As block is replaced over floral picks, apply glue to area where block and top horizontal bamboo stick touch. Allow glue to dry 15 minutes.

7. Using wire cutters, snip off ends of floral picks so they are flush with Styrofoam block.

8. Insert burgundy cherry blossom stems into block horizontally and vertically.

9. Insert white cherry blossom stems to splay out from corner, contrasting with red blossoms.

10. Insert the resin leaves for additional color and visual weight.

11. Fill in bare spots and round out floral arrangement with green hypernicum berry sprigs.

12. Carefully glue in reindeer moss to hide Styrofoam block.

13. Apply a liberal coat of pan glue to twine ball.

14. Glue the twine ball into the center of the arrangement for focal point.

How can I make a wreath from an old window or screen?

Decorating with old windows has become a very popular fashion. This project takes it a step further by adding a beautiful floral arrangement to the corner of the window, giving the illusion of a "window box."

Window Frame Wreath

Here's how:

1. Install a picture frame hanger to back of window screen.

2. Using floral knife, carve slot in Styrofoam block to fit over coving on window frame.

What you need to get started:

Tools:
- Basic tools and supplies on page 11

Materials:
- Old window screen
- Picture frame hanger
- 2½" x 4" x 1½" Styrofoam block
- Artificial ivy stems
- Artificial corkscrew willow stems
- Artificial geraniums, violets, ranunculi, iris, and tulips

Expected wreath life:
- Indefinite

Above: finished project size: 24" x 16".

3. Apply pan glue to back of Styrofoam block and stick to bottom-right corner of window frame. Allow glue to dry for 10–15 minutes so that it adheres properly.

4. Insert artificial ivy stems into block horizontally and vertically along window frame.

5. Insert artificial corkscrew willow stems horizontally and vertically across frame.
   NOTE: The artificial willow works better than real willow branches because it is more flexible and less prone to break.

6. Fill out the arrangement with artificial geraniums, violets, ranunculi, and bulb flowers such as iris and tulips. Leave some of the bulbs visible in the grouping.

7. Cover the Styrofoam block with Spanish moss. Pin the moss in place with ferning pins. Add more ivy over the moss to finish and tie the design together.

20 Project

What you need to get started:

Tools:
- Basic tools and supplies on page 11

Materials:
- 16" dia. grapevine wreath
- Artificial vine garland
- Artificial artichoke
- Artificial carrots (4)
- Artificial radishes (6)
- Artificial red kale
- Artificial stalk of celery
- Wooden spoons (3)

Expected wreath life:
- Indefinite

How can I make a wreath using a garland and a twig base?

Try using a light and airy garland to create a fabulous wreath by wrapping it around a twig base. This makes the wreath look very natural. Also, make certain to use artificial vegetables of high quality for a more "real" appearance.

Kitchen Wreath

Here's how:

1. Either purchase or make a 16" dia. grapevine wreath. (Refer to Grapevine Wreath, Steps 1–3 on pages 19–21.)

2. Attach vine garland to wreath with ferning pins.

3. Using pan glue or hot-glue gun, adhere artichoke, celery, kale, and radishes to wreath.

4. Using green-taped floral wire, tie carrots and spoons onto wreath. (Refer to Wrapped floral wire on pages 11–12.)

NOTES: To get a different range of colors in your wreath, you may wish to use artificial fruits rather than vegetables.

To make your wreath look "vintage," decorate it with heirloom kitchen utensils. Sometimes you can find these items in miniature form, which adds an extra element of charm to your wreath.

Many floral designers enjoy using glazed bread for kitchen wreaths. Glazed bread works great with any kitchen theme.

Above: finished project size: 22" diameter.

21 Project

How can I make a spray using dried materials?

The choices in dried florals today are endless. However, care must be taken when handling these materials because they tend to be quite brittle.

What you need to get started:

Tools:
- Basic tools and supplies on page 11

Materials:
- Metal-framed mirror
- 4" sq. x 2" Styrofoam block
- Dried sponge mushrooms (4)
- Dried tall wild grass stems (1 bunch)
- Artificial artichokes (2)
- Dried China millet stems (1 bunch)
- Dried jirega pods (5)
- Dried poppy pods (8)
- Dried mushroom pods (2)
- Dried setaria (1 bunch)

Expected wreath life:
- Indefinite

Mirror Spray

Here's how:

1. Cut recess into Styrofoam block to fit on frame of mirror. (Refer to Window Frame Wreath, Step 2 on page 93.)

2. Using pan glue, attach Styrofoam block to mirror frame. Because mirror frame is metal, block must also be wired onto frame with paddle wire. Allow glue to dry for 15 minutes.

3. Adhere sponge mushrooms to sides of Styrofoam block. (Refer to Pussy Willow Wreath, Step 6 on page 31.)

4. Insert tall wild grass stems as background for other foliage.

5. Layer China millet stems in front of wild grass.

6. Adhere jirega pods and poppy pods in groupings.

7. Using wire cutters, clip wire off mushroom pods and glue in place. (Refer to Western Wreath, Steps 9–10 on page 85.)

8. Adhere setaria to finish arrangement.

Above: finished project size: 18" x 26".

Section 3: Wreath Gallery

Acknowledgments

We would like to acknowledge the staff of Olive & Dahlia for their generous assistance in making wreaths for use in this book; to Taiwan Imports, Kory Fluckiger, and Doug Hatch for their creative input and loyal support.

We also wish to thank the Silver Terrace Nursery and Homes for Styling for their excellent service and superb product lines and to Doug Smith at http://wwwdougsmith.ancients. info.

Thanks also to Ted and Tiffany Woodmansee for use of their home in some of our photography.

We would also like to extend a special thank you to Jo Packham and the wonderful staff at Chapelle LTD. who made this book possible.

Lastly, we want to thank our families for the support they have so freely offered us in whatever undertaking we have made. Without their support, we would not have succeeded in our endeavors.

Metric Equivalency Chart

mm-millimeters   cm-centimeters
inches to millimeters and centimeters

inches	mm	cm	inches	cm	inches	cm
⅛	3	0.3	9	22.9	30	76.2
¼	6	0.6	10	25.4	31	78.7
⅜	10	1.0	11	27.9	32	81.3
½	13	1.3	12	30.5	33	83.8
⅝	16	1.6	13	33.0	34	86.4
¾	19	1.9	14	35.6	35	88.9
⅞	22	2.2	15	38.1	36	91.4
1	25	2.5	16	40.6	37	94.0
1¼	32	3.2	17	43.2	38	96.5
1½	38	3.8	18	45.7	39	99.1
1¾	44	4.4	19	48.3	40	101.6
2	51	5.1	20	50.8	41	104.1
2½	64	6.4	21	53.3	42	106.7
3	76	7.6	22	55.9	43	109.2
3½	89	8.9	23	58.4	44	111.8
4	102	10.2	24	61.0	45	114.3
4½	114	11.4	25	63.5	46	116.8
5	127	12.7	26	66.0	47	119.4
6	152	15.2	27	68.6	48	121.9
7	178	17.8	28	71.1	49	124.5
8	203	20.3	29	73.7	50	127.0

About the Authors

After their first meeting in 1976, Pat Poce and Deon Gooch partnered together to open The Posy Place in Ogden, Utah. Since then, they have become leaders in the floral industry.

Pat has served as chairman of Telfora, Northwest Florists' Association, Utah Allied Florists, and FTD Association conventions. Deon, seeing the possibility in items usually passed over, specializes in procuring raw materials for use in floral designs. Sharing his vision with Pat, they have combined their talents to produce highly innovative and unique floral designs.

Pat and Deon have participated with various design teams to provide floral arrangements for several national events, including: a White House Reception hosted by President and Mrs. Reagan, the Statue of Liberty Restoration Celebration, the 1993 Inauguration of President Clinton, and the 1996 Summer Olympics in Atlanta.

Always striving to take their floral designs to new levels in both scope and size, Pat and Deon recently opened a new floral venture—Olive & Dahlia. Set on Ogden's Historic 25th Street, it has enlarged the scale of floral display to include fountains, arbors, wreaths, and creative floral groupings. Their artistic and imaginative designs have been recognized both in the community and the floral industry.

Having found fulfillment in their careers as floral designers and by writing a book on basic floral design, Pat and Deon hope to grant the reader useful techniques that can bring the art of floral design into any home, for any taste, and within the reach of any budget.

Index